EFFECTIVE PLANNING
FOR
BETTER SCHOOL BUILDINGS

EFFECTIVE PLANNING
FOR
BETTER SCHOOL BUILDINGS

JAMES M. THRASHER

PENDELL
PUBLISHING
COMPANY

International Standard Book Number: 0-87812-048-3
Library of Congress Catalog Card Number: 72-93769

CONTENTS

PREFACE

It is the intention of this publication to set a framework for attacking the school facilities planning process. The framework established for each individual project will vary from place to place and with the complexity of the planning problem. Nevertheless, there is great need for the various roles to be played to be understood by all involved.

If this document can assist school boards, school administrators, teachers, and architects to clearly identify and understand their part in the drama of planning functional school facilities, it will have achieved the goals set for it by the author.

INTRODUCTION

PLANNING FOR BETTER SCHOOL BUILDINGS

Planning is a magic word. It opens the gate to progress. Without planning the question cannot be answered as to where we are going or how to get there. Aimless wandering may be appropriate for some leisure time activities where no known objectives exist other than to enjoy the environment of the moment. On the other hand, if there are objectives to be attained, not only must the word "planning" be prominent in our minds, but the process of planning must be implemented. The technology of our modern world could not exist if industry and business had not planned exceedingly well. The modern jet airliner is not an accident. Careful planning charted each step of the development process. Engineers carefully considered speed, safety, ground handling characteristics, support services, and passenger comfort in arriving at recommended design. There is ample evidence that our great air transportation industry is still reaching out to make air travel safer and even more efficient.

The seriousness and complexity of providing functional instructional spaces in a modern school facility creates a tremendous need for planning. The impact on the local school community of providing the financial resources is almost always a factor to be reckoned with. Therefore, we cannot afford the wastefulness inherent in a lack of planning. The obligation to provide the learners and their managers (the teachers) with facilities that enhance the learning process is a paramount responsibility. Planning for schools must be given as much or more attention than we would expect in the development of new improved vehicles for air transportation. As the last brick is placed in the new school facility, the decisions that were made in the planning stages are nearly as irrevocable as the moment when the airline captain reaches the point of V_{mc} (velocity, minimum control) and commits the ship to flight.

The magnitude of the task in providing new and replacement instructional space in America's schools is almost overwhelming. One set of enrollment projections of students in the elementary grades

1

indicates a need for 40,700 additional instructional spaces (classrooms) by 1980.[1] The same projection forecasts a need for 161,000 new instructional spaces for high school youth by 1980. The growing need for additional facilities is almost overshadowed by the growing obsolescence of school space now in use. The latest report on schools indicates that 215,000 classrooms now in use were built before 1920. Over 41,000 of these older buildings are constructed of combustible materials.[2]

The growing need for additional space and for replacement of instructional space can be easily documented. It amounts to almost a national tragedy that each day communities tax themselves for new school facilities, build the building only to have a facility that is thirty years out of date the moment it is opened. A few schools achieve recognition for their functional planning. For each one singled out as an exemplary model there are dozens that are just like the school house constructed in the 1940's. The advancing technology available on the educational scene, the new approaches to "adaptable scheduling," the cooperative approaches of more than one teacher in the instructional process, and the use of "open space" dictate a new look. The school facilities to house today's instructional program must be as innovative as the programs that are to be carried on within the designed spaces.

---

1 Population estimates, U.S. Department of Commerce, Series P-25, No. 365, May 5, 1967.
2 Digest of Educational Statistics, 1967 Edition, U.S. Department of Health Education and Welfare. OE-10024-67, p. 48.

THE PLANNING PROCESS
— as it once was —

School planning of yesterday was most often approached by the local board of education and the school administrator as being essentially an architectural problem. A meager amount of hard data was supplied to give the architect some parameters within which to operate. Usual data supplied would specify the number of students to be housed, the grades involved, and the total amount of the funds available for the construction of the school building.

The architect, armed with this basic information, would retreat to his drawing board and proceed to establish the design for the new school building. He was thus forced into a role of deciding how to establish instructional space, its potential use, and essentially the function of the school as it was shaped by the bricks and mortar of its outside shell.

THE LONELY SCHOOL ARCHITECT OF YESTERYEAR

THE PLANNING PROCESS
— as it should be —

Schools exist for the purpose of carrying out instructional tasks. The main players in the drama are the students. Teachers are supporting cast and the professional technicians in directing the activities, determining the resources to be used, and the sequence of events in the learning-teaching process.

Boards of directors in local school districts are charged with the responsibility for establishing broad policy guides for the curriculum of their schools. They hold the chief executive officer, the school superintendent, responsible for overall program implementation and fiscal planning. The architect plays a key part in the school planning process *after* certain professional determinations have been made.

In the last few years an additional person has appeared on the school planning scene. This is the school facilities planning consultant. School districts may not be large enough to have full time professional staff people in this capacity and often contract with colleges or universities for this kind of service. There are several private firms which render service to schools and colleges in the planning consultant role.

School districts have too much at stake when undertaking the important task of planning for new schools to not exert every effort to obtain the best facility possible. The team approach to the planning venture is an absolute must if the patrons are to really get their money's worth in the new school facilities.

SCHOOL PLANNING COLLAGE

A TEAM PROCESS

ARCHITECT

CONSULTANTS

SCHOOL

SUPERINTENDENT

TEACHERS

SCHOOL BOARDS

COMMUNITIES

THE TEACHER'S ROLE
IN THE PLANNING PROCESS

The classroom teacher has a unique contribution to make in the school planning process. She is the practitioner who will work directly in fashioning and guiding the learning activities of children. Each teacher individually may not be able to contribute to the total role that should be the realm of the teachers' world. However, a teacher, a group of teachers, and special instructional resource people will be able to fulfill the needed and expected role of the teacher in school planning.

The educational specifications must contain quite a detailed explanation or description of just what activities students will be engaged in as they seek to carry on pursuit of knowledge. This description of student activities needs to be developed to an extensive and explicit degree. It is through the word picture thus painted that the architect can visualize what it is that must be planned for in terms of physical space. It is important for him to know whether students are expected to all be doing the same thing at a given time or if some students will be engaged in one activity while others are busy at other tasks.

No less important is a description of the activities of the teacher in the classroom, the learning laboratory, or in other facilities within the school plant. The physical facilities, called the school house, should be planned and constructed in such a way that the building is a supporting player in the drama of the learning environment enhancing the efforts of the teacher to create the optimum conditions for learning.

Very often teachers assume that when asked to participate in the planning for new schools that they should specify how much drawer space or shelving they should have or some equally fixed accessory. Instead of pursuing their job in assisting the planning by detailing storage requirements, they should spend their efforts in describing the materials and resources they and their students will be using. She must also specify on what basis certain equipment is to be used and by whom. The architect is then in a position to put his specialized skill to work in devising adequate storage space so that things are close to where they will be used and readily available if this is what is needed. The example of the art teacher will serve to illustrate this point. This person had seven different sizes of art paper in five different colors for which she needed storage. She spent many hours attempting to arrange a drawing showing drawer space needed to store the paper. She was finally convinced that she should simply list the sizes of paper to be stored and in what quantity and how often students were to have access to it. The architect very quickly arranged a slanted multiple layered bin that provided the needed paper storage.

The classroom teacher and special instructional resource people in the school district have another contribution to make in facilities planning. The architect cannot be and should not try to be an educational crystal ball gazer as to the future direction of educational practice. The teacher and her co-workers must set forth in a written form the trends in program development that they see. This responsibility carries with it the mandate to make sure they are current in their thinking about trends. They should examine new research findings and promising practices aboard in the land in order that they not be guilty of perpetuating the status quo when new developments have rendered changes in curriculum or educational practices.

TEACHER ROLE IN PLANNING

- DESCRIBE STUDENT ACTIVITIES

- DESCRIBE TEACHER ACTIVITIES

- DESCRIBE RESOURCES TO BE
            UTILIZED

- DESCRIBE PROGRAM DEVELOPMENTS

THE SCHOOL ADMINISTRATOR'S ROLE
IN THE PLANNING PROCESS

The school administrator has a very definite and important role to play in school facilities planning. As the executive responsible for administering school operations, he must have a broad perspective of the school program. He is the chief advisor and resource person to the board of education. This responsibility carries with it the job of program development overview. This responsibility is interpreted to mean that he must examine the work of the teacher planning groups and work with the consultants to see that the written descriptions of program reflect the proper balance of emphasis and are consistent with the educational objectives of that school and that community. He cannot escape this responsibility. In the final analysis he must recommend the educational specifications to the board as representing the program that will best fulfill the educational hopes and aspirations of the school and the community which it serves.

The school superintendent has another task assigned by virtue of his position as chief executive of the board of education. He must work with the architect and the consultants in interpretation of the educational specifications. This interpretive task includes review of the specifications with the architect as he works to clear up questions that might occur or to assist in the visualization of educational activity. The main interpretation function, however, is to review the plans at various stages of development to insure that they do follow the written word descriptions provided by the educational specifications. This review implies that at the appropriate times the superintendent will recommend to the board the acceptance of the architect's plans with the assurance that they do adequately portray the intent of the educational specifications.

As chief advisor and resource person to the board of education, the superintendent is responsible for fiscal management. This entails planning for bond issues, special tax levies, state financial aid or combinations of these that will be necessary to bring the facilities planning venture to fruition in the form of a school plant. The fiscal planning will involve the architect for the project since material costs, amount of space to be provided, unusual building problems associated with weather or available manpower will influence the final cost figures. The superintendent must be in a position to advise the board that the plans for the school facilities and the fiscal plans are in harmony as *estimated* by the known facts at the time bids are advertised.

11

SCHOOL ADMINISTRATOR'S ROLE

- PROGRAM DEVELOPMENT OVERVIEW

- PLAN REVIEW

- FISCAL RESPONSIBILITY

THE BOARD OF EDUCATION
(TRUSTEE'S) ROLE

The board of education occupies a position of extreme sensitivity in the planning for new school facilities. By the very nature of the activity they must set the wheels in motion. The decision to plan for additional facilities or to operate on the status quo must be based on facts and educational program aspirations. Information as to needs, both short range and long range, should be supplied through the chief administration of the school district. Upon the facts that are known and the educational implications of the action the board must reach the decision as to whether new school facilities are needed. The board of education must authorize the project if in their policy decision making role they deem it in the best interests of their community that new facilities be planned.

A community or city cannot operate local government functions of a complex nature with all individuals participating in decision making except at the time elections are in order. The board of education stands in the place of the citizen group to render action in their behalf. One action that the school board takes that has a far reaching influence on the life of the community is in the selection of an architect for a new facilities project. The actual role of the architect will be dealt with later. At this point the extreme importance of making a wise decision on the employment of the professional architect must be emphasized. The board will undoubtedly explore the avenues of information about potential architects or firms of architects that might be superior candidates for this most important trust. The board is the legal "owner" of the school and as such employs the architect who will work with them and others to bring about the planning and construction of the new school facilities.

The complexity of the modern world has also affected the school planning process. There are many facets of the problem to be explored, discussed, and finally settled upon or discarded. During the planning time, the local administrators usually have their regular duties to perform. It is asking more than can be expected of the busy superintendent, or the school principal, to attend to all of the details of educational planning for the new project. Many school boards are finding that it is expedient as well as wise to employ educational consultants for school planning from outside the district to work with the local school groups, the board, and the architect. Educational consultants for school planning can bring a wealth of information and

stimulus to school program development. Their opportunity to participate in many planning projects increases the potential for the local
school to capitalize on previous experience and know-how. The board
of education must weigh the importance of detailed educational
planning and to employ outside educational planning assistance if they
deem it in the best interests of their school district.

Most people have considerable pride in their abilities. This is a
natural human trait. School board members are leaders in their
community or else they would not be elected representatives of the
people on the board. It is understandable that board members often
consider themselves as somewhat knowledgeable about construction or
planning and project themselves into a dubious position in the school
planning role. The board member is not the architect doing the
architectural planning. He is not the professional teacher participating
in "painting" the word picture of the educational activities to be
accommodated in the new structure. The wise board member will
participate unofficially in the planning process. He listens to the
development of program ideas and the resultant potential building
ramifications. He asks questions for understanding in order to be able
to interpret developments in the process to his fellow citizens. His role
at this point is an unofficial one for the building of understanding upon
which later official decisions may be based.

As the "owner" of the building, the board must reach a decision as
to the appropriateness of the architectural plans for the structure.
Ideally, the board might consider their official sanction of the planning
process. The first designated decision point could advantageously be set
at the schematic idea stage. The schematic idea plan is the architect's
production of a simple relationship diagram that translates the
educational program planning into a workable scheme. The relation-
ships between various functions of the facility is the important concept
of this stage. The board should review the preliminary plans prepared
by the architect as the second decision point in official approval. At
this stage the basic plans are set, the square footage of the new building
is established, and the most important question asked and answered.
"Does the plan meet the needs as to function as outlined in the
educational specifications to be able to implement the program
envisaged?" The third and final decision point in the board review of
plans comes at the time for approval of final plans and specifications.
This responsibility for plan approval cannot be delegated away.

The Board of Education (Trustee's) Role

The board of education has the role of judge to fill at the time that the board must exercise its judgment as to the adequacy of the funds available to meet the bid prices and if the bids are in the best interest of the district in pushing the project on to completion. The award of bids is the prerogative and the responsibility of the board of education.

BOARD OF EDUCATION ROLE

- AUTHORIZE THE PROJECT

- HIRE THE ARCHITECT

- EMPLOY CONSULTANTS

- PARTICIPATE UNOFFICIALLY IN PLANNING

- OFFICIAL RESPONSIBILITY FOR PLANS

- FINAL APPROVAL OF THE PROJECT

THE EDUCATIONAL CONSULTANT ROLE

The quality of the contribution that the outside educational consultant can render to a school facilities planning project will be directly related to his understanding and knowledge of program and instruction. In addition, he must have a thorough understanding of the process of planning and the respective roles of the personnel involved in that process. Experience in working with architects in interpretation of educational needs is a most valuable asset. The school agency that employs an outside educational consultant should consider carefully the quality of the service that is being purchased.

Not every school district contemplating a planning project will want to employ an educational consultant. However, if the board of education wants to provide their community with the very best educational facility for the dollars expended, they must not fail to recognize the need for planning service. They may make a decision to free some administrator within the system to carry out the coordination of the planning function. In most cases boards would be well advised to consider outside consultants for at least three reasons. School administrators within the district already have full time duties in the operation of the school. It is difficult to free them from existing assignments. The majority of school administrators have had little or no experience in the planning process. The consultant from outside can be a valuable source of new ideas and suggestions. They are often able to push back the curtain on the educational horizon and assist local school personnel in seeing the educational implications of a better school program and the facilities needed to implement these programs. Whether the educational consultant is employed from outside the district or someone is assigned the special duty from within, the role of such a person must be fulfilled.

The educational consultant is charged with the responsibility for the coordination of the planning effort. He should lay out a plan of action or sequence of events to carry through the complete planning process cycle. The shorter the time element for planning, the more critical is the timing of the planning of mile-stone event occurrence. The coordination must take into account the complexity of the program to be accommodated in the new facilities, the number of teachers and other school personnel that should be involved, and the liaison with citizens' groups to build understanding of the educational program development and needed facilities to house that program.

The educational consultant must be adept at working with groups or individual faculty members. The ideas on instruction and trends in specialized fields that faculty can and may contribute must not be minimized. It is necessary for the consultant to contribute ideas to spark discussion and broaden the base of instructional considerations in each field as the draft of educational specifications is being built. The educational consultant cannot be an accomplished authority in all fields. He, therefore, may elect to add a specialist in a given area to the planning discussion who is really an extension of himself to accomplish the objective of widening horizons in one or two work sessions on a specific topic.

It is easy for strong divisions, groups of teachers, or departments to influence the thinking of those at the center of the school planning venture. It must be remembered that schools are planned for the purpose of instruction of people. Facilities should not be planned for the convenience of one teacher or a special interest group. The educational consultant plays a vital role in making program suggestions that lead to a balanced program consideration. It is his job to examine total program needs and to draw attention to areas that are being given less than adequate attention or that are being given more attention in terms of space consideration than is warranted by the nature of the instruction to be carried on in that space.

School people usually find it easier to talk about the program involved in planning for the new school than to get a description of it down on paper. This is a function of the educational consultant. It is his obligation to work with the various groups in talking about the program and then see to it that program development, ideas on instruction, and actual needs of each program area are put in writing. This task must be accomplished. The written description of each instructional area and the relationship to each other are the educational specifications from which the architect can plan space enclosed by brick and mortar to accommodate and enhance the learning experiences to be conducted within. The educational specifications should truly be a vivid word picture of the activities of students and teachers to guide the architect in the design of the new school facility.

The experienced educational consultant can perform a valuable service in assisting the architect in the interpretation of the educational specifications. The architect cannot fulfill the role of being an expert in the field of education. Most architects will welcome the opportunity to have an experienced school planning specialist to converse with, to use as a sounding board, and finally to assist in evaluation of plan ideas as to adequacy in meeting the educational specifications as written.

CONSULTANT ROLE

- COORDINATE PLANNING EFFORT

- IDEA STIMULATORS

- PROGRAM SUGGESTIONS

- WRITING DUTY

- ASSIST ARCHITECT IN EDUCATIONAL
  SPECIFICATION INTERPRETATION

THE ARCHITECT'S ROLE

A creative and skillful architect is a must if all the careful educational planning is to bear fruit in the form of a building designed to house the described program. The architect uses his skill and imagination to fashion enclosures of space that lend dignity, beauty, and functionalism to the total school. Each school building project should be created as a new and distinct problem to be solved. American architects have been willing to expend tremendous effort to improve the quality of school design and at the same time keep school building costs below other comparable business and industrial building costs.

The first task of the architect is to become thoroughly familiar with the written educational specifications. It is only through this written word that he can begin to form some feel for the project as an entity. The educational specifications form the foundation for the architectural development of a schematic idea for the building. This schematic is not drawn to scale or outlined walls and designation of square footage. The schematic is a dream of relationship of space to space or function of the various components of the total school plant. It is the development of relationship of site and terrain to the building as well as the integral parts of the school building. It is recommended that the board of education review and approve the schematic idea for the proposed new building.

At the preliminary plan stage the architect places each of the component parts of the building in place and allocates space to each function on a scaled basis. The preliminary plans grow out of the schematic idea of the structure and the details of the educational specifications. Adequate time must be given to the development of the preliminary plans to insure adequacy in meeting the program needs as expressed in writing. These plans should be examined in light of the educational specifications in some detail. The board of education should review the preliminary plans and approve them. It is unrealistic to expect or demand major changes following the approval of the preliminary plans.

The major design work for the new building will be accomplished in the schematic idea and preliminary plan stage. Final plans and specifications take time and effort of the skilled architect, structural engineer, electrical engineer, acoustical engineer, and mechanical engineer. The many details of the building must be handled and included in plans and specifications. There has been much misunderstanding about the architectural service costs in school construction.

Much of the misunderstanding is lack of information on the part played by the supporting cast of specialists that do detail work on the plans and specifications such as the electrical and mechanical engineers. The architect is responsible for presenting the final plans and specifications to the board of education for their approval and authorization to proceed to issue the call for bids.

The architect's role has not been completed when bids have been received. During the entire construction phase and up to final inspection and acceptance of the building, the architect acts as the agent of the school district to supervise construction. He is responsible for seeing to the adequacy of performance on the part of the contractor. In cases of dispute, the architect must represent the district in insuring that the specifications on which the contractor agreed to work are carried out. An architect or architectural firm should be considered for employment by a school district with their history of proper supervision being one of the criteria.

ARCHITECT'S ROLE

- SCHEMATIC IDEA

- PRELIMINARY PLANS

- FINAL PLANS

- SUPERVISE CONSTRUCTION

THE COMMUNITY ROLE IN
PLANNING FOR SCHOOL BUILDINGS

Schools belong to the community. They are established by and for the people who reside within the boundaries of a given school district. Although the state has the responsibility for education in a constitutional sense, they have delegated the major responsibilities to the local school district via a local elected board of education.

The broad purposes of education are established by the citizens in the school district. As long as they meet the minimum standards established by law for the state the local school district may establish programs to fit their needs and wishes. The citizens within the geographic bonds of the school district are influential in establishing the purposes of their schools either directly or through the elected board of education.

Community residents must understand the need for new school buildings. It is only through such understanding that they can be in a logical position to support a building program both psychologically and emotionally.

Citizens are acutely aware of the cost of education in the 1970's. School buildings are very visible items in a community. As a result they are often praised or castigated. If the general public knows the planning process that has led to the construction of a new school plant, they may have developed a feel for the structure which is to serve them. A lack of knowledge about the planning process and the educational program implication which dictated the form of the building or buildings can only lead to misunderstanding as to why a school building was planned in such a way.

The time table for planning and construction of a new school building takes between one and two years. Very often the residents of a school district vote a bond issue or a special tax levy for new construction and are extremely disappointed when the facilities are not immediately forthcoming. In some cases the need for additional facilities or replacement of classrooms dictates that another election for financing buildings be held before those voted in the last election can be finished. Unless there is wide understanding on the part of the general citizenry on what a realistic time table is for planning and construction for new school plants there is most apt to be confusion and some lack of enthusiasm for subsequent building programs.

The community sets the tone for education. The hopes and aspirations for educational opportunity for their children and for themselves held by the citizens of a school district will ultimately determine the direction of education in that school district.

Citizens groups should be organized to participate in the planning effort. It is imperative at the outset that such citizens groups understand the whole planning process and recognize that planning is done by describing the curriculum or program to be housed. Parents and citizens are ordinarily not the experts in this field. Their participation may well be labelled as unofficial since they have no direct expertise in program development and have no legal responsibility as do the board of education. This "unofficial" participation does not imply that there is not a need for such involvement or that it is not an important function. Through the participation of the citizens group can come more understanding of the total school program. In some instances the citizens group may serve as a sounding board for new or improved program development and its appropriateness and receptivity at a given point in time.

Community groups hold the key to financing new schools. The major portion of all school building finance arrangements rests on bond issues and/or special levy elections. The community decides whether or not it intends to support the building program through the ballot box. The involvement of citizens groups at the outset in the planning process, their awareness of need, their understanding of the projected educational program for which space was needed, is most likely to insure that they will support the financing plans to bring the building program to fruition.

COMMUNITY ROLE IN PLANNING FOR SCHOOL PLANTS

- ASSIST IN ESTABLISHING THE SCHOOL'S BROAD PURPOSES

- UNDERSTAND THE NEED FOR NEW SCHOOL PLANT

- UNDERSTAND THE PLANNING PROCESS FOR THE NEW SCHOOL

- BE AWARE OF THE TIME TABLE FOR PLANNING AND CONSTRUCTION

- VOICE HOPES AND ASPIRATIONS FOR EDUCATION IN THE COMMUNITY

- PARTICIPATE AS A CITIZEN'S GROUP IN UNOFFICIAL PLANNING

- SUPPORT THE FINANCING PLAN FOR NEW SCHOOLS

THE ROLE OF STUDENTS IN PLANNING FOR NEW SCHOOL BUILDINGS

The role that students might play in the planning process for new school buildings has generally been overlooked by the majority of school planners and school administrators. This may be the result of being unaware of the potential contribution that students can make. It is true that the student group at any one time is a transient one. The four years that a single student spends in a school facility is a relatively short portion of the life expectancy of the school plant. On the other hand, the student is the client for which schools exist. A study of student needs and actual participation of those students old enough to understand the planning process can yield rich rewards in contribution and insight into the total planning effort and will certainly contribute to a sense of pride and student identity with "their" school.

Students of junior and senior high school age can participate directly on the planning team. Representatives from student government or specially designated students to participate along with the teachers, community members, and board members is in order. The designated student representatives on the planning team need to develop a system of communication to the larger student group in order to facilitate a flow of information, ideas, and the planning progress. It is imperative that the students involved understand the total planning progress and the part that they are expected to play in it.

Students on the planning team can contribute to the needed information on special student needs. These should be in the same format of program or activity description's that permeates all of the educational planning phase for new school buildings. Students are in a unique position as primary users of the school plant to indicate areas of existing programs that appear to be lacking or have been especially meaningful to the student group. They are able to communicate program needs for consideration when new programs are to be considered.

Student life in and around school buildings can be enhanced or impeded just as the cognitive learning effort can be slowed down by inadequate facilities. Student representatives on the planning team can make a contribution in pinpointing student needs that merit consideration for the student activities areas of the school. The areas for student government, after school functions, and adjunct physical recreation areas should reflect some of the thinking of the student population.

Students form a direct link to the community. It has been generally accepted that a communication link does exist from the school to the home via the student. There probably has always existed a flow of information via students to a wider group in the community outside the students own family. This linkage may exist through youth organizations, through church groups, and any other organization where youth and adults come into contact. A less formal line of communication exists within the community between students and adults through the daily contacts in business establishments that serve any of the needs of youth. The attitude toward school and its activities is transmitted from student to adult. Excitement, understanding, and enthusiasm for planning for new school facilities may well be communicated from students to people in the community if the student group is involved in the planning process in a meaningful manner.

THE ROLE OF STUDENTS IN PLANNING FOR NEW SCHOOL BUILDINGS

- PARTICIPATE ON THE PLANNING TEAM

- PROVIDE INFORMATION ON SPECIAL STUDENT NEEDS

- ASSIST IN PROGRAM FORMULATION FOR ACTIVITIES AREAS

- REFLECT STUDENT VIEW OF NEEDS TO THE COMMUNITY

CONCLUSION

The investment of financial resources in school facilities within a community is now a sizeable one. The next twenty years will bring no appreciable diminution in the overall need to keep up or increase the pace for school buildings to meet increased enrollments and to replace obsolete instructional spaces. School facilities are a community asset and a resource, but they do cost money. The question each community and each school board must ask itself is, "Can we do less than exert every human effort to insure that our school facilities are the best that can be planned and developed to enhance the learning environment for our most important resource, our young people?"

The planning process as described through the exploration of the roles of the people involved in the school will bring closer the dream of obtaining the ultimate in functional design for new school buildings.

This publication emphasizes that citizens, students, and teachers, as well as architects and administrators, should be actively involved in planning for school buildings. This involvement is essential in order that school plants serve their purpose; facilitating learning.

Participation in planning helps to insure financial support and intelligent use of buildings when they are completed. A strong plea is made for provision for enough planning time for thinking and discussion of the kinds of programs curriculum and experiences, for which the facilities are needed.

Acceptance and implementation of the concepts that are emphasized in this book, i.e., facility planning as an integral part of curriculum development and all of those affected by the school program to be involved in planning, will do much to strengthen American education.

ROBERT S. GILCHRIST, Ph.D.
Professor of Education

United States International University
San Diego, California